D1084627

How I Pack My Lunch

by Jennifer Boothroyd

first step nonfiction

Lerner Publications Company · Minneapolis

LERNER

e

SOURCE

Expand learning beyond the printed book. Download free, complementary educational resources for this book from our website, www.lernerresource.com.

Copyright © 2014 by Lerner Publishing Group, Inc.

All rights reserved. International copyright secured. No part of this book may be reproduced, stored in a retrieval system, or transmitted in any form or by any means—electronic, mechanical, photocopying, recording, or otherwise—without the prior written permission of Lerner Publishing Group, Inc., except for the inclusion of brief quotations in an acknowledged review.

The images in this book are used with the permission of: © Todd Strand/Independent Picture Service.

Front Cover: © Todd Strand/Independent Picture Service.

Main body text set in ITC Avant Garde Gothic Std Medium 21/25.
Typeface provided by Adobe Systems.

Lerner Publications Company
A division of Lerner Publishing Group, Inc.
241 First Avenue North
Minneapolis, MN 55401 USA

For reading levels and more information, look up this title at www.lernerbooks.com.

Library of Congress Cataloging-in-Publication Data

Boothroyd, Jennifer, 1972–
    How I pack my lunch / by Jennifer Boothroyd.
        pages cm. — (First step nonfiction—responsibility in action)
    Includes index.
    ISBN 978–1–4677–3635–0 (lib. bdg. : alk. paper)
    ISBN 978–1–4677–3653–4 (eBook)
    1. Lunchbox cooking—Juvenile literature. I. Title.
TX735.B66 2014
641.5'3—dc23   2013031507

Manufactured in the United States of America
1 – BP – 12/31/13

Table of Contents

I'm packing my lunch
for school.

Where should I start?

First, I get out my water bottle.

I fill my bottle with cold water.

Next, I get out my
lunch box.

Making a Sandwich

Then I decide what I want
to eat.

I get out lettuce, turkey, cheese, and two **slices** of bread.

I make a lettuce, turkey, and cheese **sandwich**.

I put my sandwich in
a **container**.

Next, I put carrots in a container.

I put grapes in a container.

I get a **napkin**.

Then I get out an
ice pack.

Finally, I put everything
inside my lunch box.

That's how I packed my lunch.

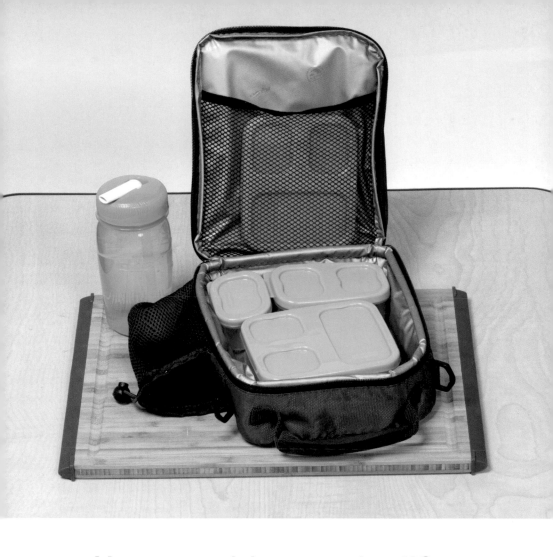

How would you do it?

Activity

Write a Story

Pretend that you are responsible for packing your lunch for school tomorrow. On a separate sheet of paper, write a story about the steps that you would take to do this job. Use at least three of the words shown on the opposite page to write your story.

Story Word List

first

next

then

last

before

after

finally

Fun Facts

- Around 150 years ago, many children brought lunch to school in small metal pails. These days, many kids use vinyl or plastic lunch boxes.

- A healthful lunch includes fruits, vegetables, whole grains, dairy, and protein. Protein is in foods such as turkey, fish, and nuts.

- Cold lunches should be kept cold. Use ice packs if you can't put your lunch in a refrigerator.

Glossary

container – a box, a jar, or a bowl that holds something

lunch box – a container used to carry a small meal

napkin – paper or cloth used to clean the mouth and hands

sandwich – slices of bread or a roll with meat, cheese, or other fillings

slices – thin, flat pieces cut from something

Index